2024
VISION BOARD CLIP ART BOOK FOR
WOMEN

This Book Includes 150 + Images, Quotes and Affirmations Words in all areas of life below.

What are you waiting for?

Create Your Powerful Vision Borad and Manifest Your Dreams

Health & Fitness

- Lose Weight
- Nutrition
- Workout
- Learn To Swim

Relationships goals

- Friendship
- Wedding
- Family
- Pregnancy

Travel Goals

- New Places
- Learn To Surf
- Road Trip

Mindset Spirit

- Reading
- Self Care

Things you Want To own

- Dream House
- Dream Car
- Makeup
- Clothes

Hobbies

- Photography
- Dance
- Shopping

Healthy
Food

BODY
UNDER
CONSTRUCTION

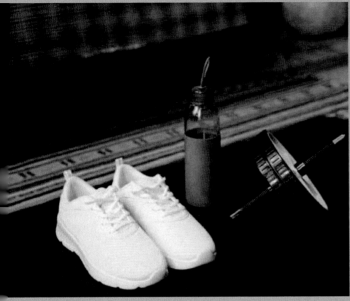

I'M WORKING OUT NOT TO BE SKINNY BUT TO BE FIT

Just
Keep
Swimming

All I
Want
To Do Is
Swim

Friends

If Lost Or
DRUNK
—PLEASE—
return to
FRIEND

Your
Friendship
Means
The World
To Me

You Will Forever Be My Always

Just Married

Family
Where Life
Begins and
Love
Never Ends

Family The
Important Thing
In The World

I Have a
Great

Family

BES
T
MOM
EVER

ALL
MY
LOVE

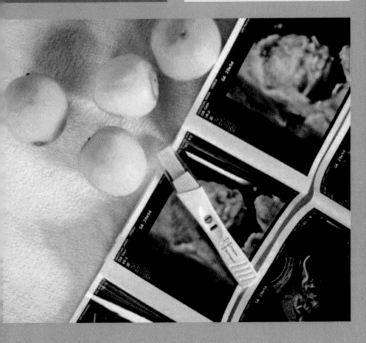

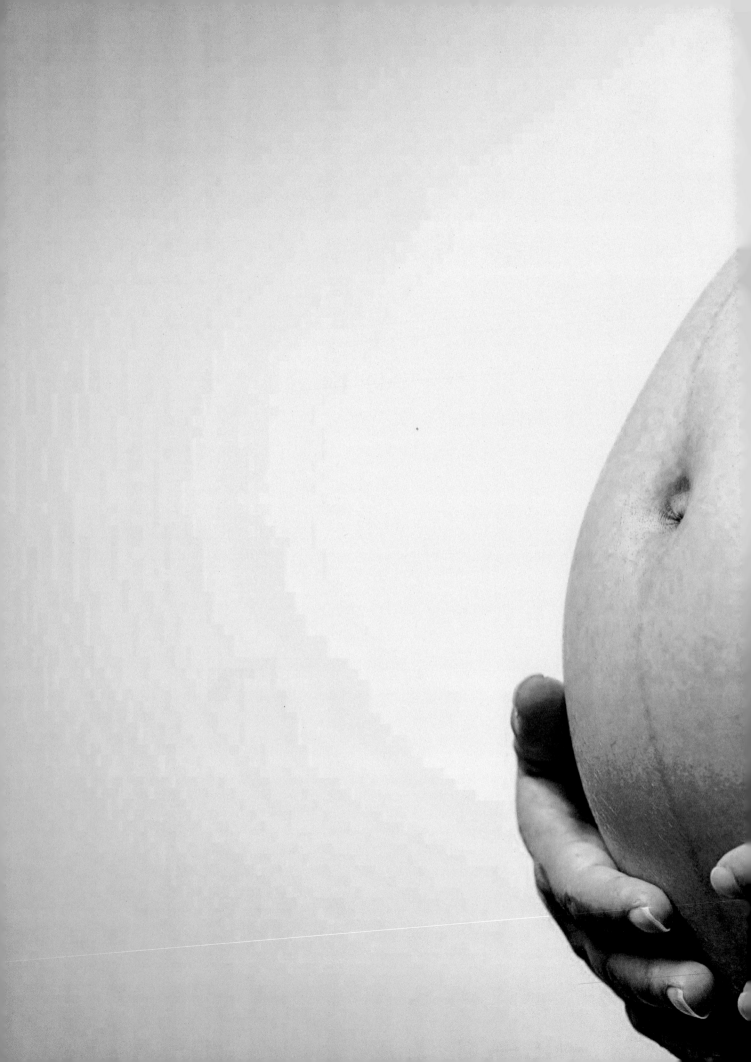

AJ

Life IS BETTER WHEN You -SURF-

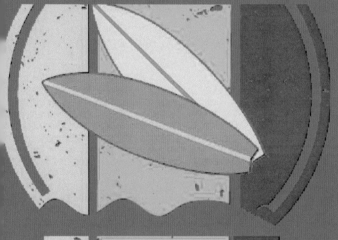

SURFER GIRL

You Can't Stop The Waves But You Can Learn To Surf

It's Time For a New Adventure

So Much World So Little Time

DON'T STOP READING

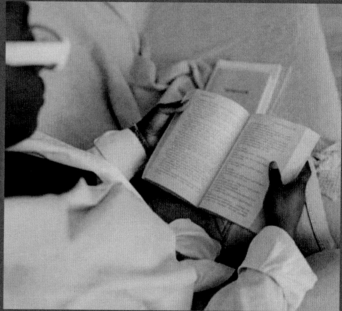

Reading is Never a Waste Of Time

This
Girl
Loves To
Dance

Just
Dance

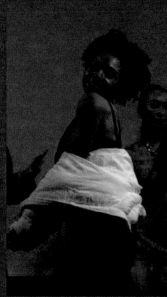

Follow Your Dreams

DO WHAT YOU LOVE

HAPPINESS IS RECEIVING WHAT YOU ORDERERD ONLINE

SALE 20% OFF

I Could Give Up Shopping But I am Not a Quitter

Made in the USA
Las Vegas, NV
26 November 2024

12671824R00026